The Mute

Waves whisper secrets to the shore,
Softly crashing, forevermore.
The sea breathes out a lullaby,
Underneath the dimming sky.

Colors blend in twilight's hue,
A silent dance of night and blue.
The moon hangs low, a guiding light,
As shadows weave through the night.

Lifting Layers

Petals stretch, reaching high,
Unfolding dreams beneath the sky.
The dawn peeks through the veil of night,
Inviting all to share its light.

Gentle breezes, whispers low,
Nature's art begins to show.
Each layer kissed by morning's hand,
Awakens life across the land.

Softly Unfolding

Quiet moments wrapped in time,
Nature's rhythm, a soothing chime.
A bud reveals its quiet might,
As colors bloom in morning light.

Each breeze carries a tale unspoken,
In whispers sweet, and hearts wide open.
The world exhales, a tender sigh,
As dreams take wing and learn to fly.

Graceful Awakenings

The sky blushes at dawn's embrace,
Filling the world with gentle grace.
Each heartbeat echoes pure delight,
As day breaks through the tender night.

Awake, the fields in golden bloom,
Banish shadows, dispel the gloom.
Life bursts forth in vibrant hues,
With every step, the heart renews.

Lifting Through Quietude

In stillness, whispers call,
Ancient echoes softly fall.
Moments linger, a breath long,
Harmony within the song.

Shadows dance beneath the trees,
Carried softly by the breeze.
Hearts align, the world slows down,
In silence, wear the crown.

Time unfolds in gentle grace,
Each heartbeat finds its place.
Between the thoughts, peace flows wide,
In quietude, we abide.

Stars emerge, the night unveils,
Dreams awaken, love prevails.
In the calm, our spirits rise,
Lifting through the painted skies.

With every step, the ground is light,
Guided by the moon's soft light.
In this space, we're ever free,
Quietude, our remedy.

The Stealthy Path to Growth

In shadows, roots entwine deep,
Silent promise, secrets keep.
From the earth, a rise unknown,
Courage blooms where winds have blown.

Each small step, a choice it makes,
Through the darkness, daylight breaks.
Paths of whispers, tales untold,
In the silence, dreams unfold.

Time moves slow, yet ever fast,
Lessons learned from moments past.
Every branch, a story weaves,
Stealthy growth, in hearts, believes.

Nature's rhythm guides the way,
Brick by brick, we learn to sway.
Underneath, the strength will show,
From the roots, the rise will grow.

In the stillness, courage finds,
Open hearts and open minds.
The stealthy path, a treasure trove,
In quiet strength, we learn to move.

Embers in the Dark

Flickers glow in the midnight air,
Softly speaking, stories rare.
All around, shadows reside,
In the dark, the dreams confide.

Whispers linger, secrets shared,
Hidden hopes are lightly bared.
Embers dance within the night,
Guiding souls with gentle light.

Through the silence, echoes hum,
Heartbeats in the dark, a drum.
Each spark tells of battles fought,
From the ashes, wisdom sought.

Underneath the moonlit sky,
Potent dreams begin to fly.
Embers glow with strength imbued,
In the dark, our spirits renewed.

With each flicker, futures gleam,
Fragments of a waking dream.
In darkness, let the light ignite,
Embers bright, our endless fight.

The Secret Ascendant

Beneath the surface, power lies,
Hidden pathways to the skies.
Quiet strength that dares to rise,
In shadows, light begins to prize.

Gentle winds, a silent force,
Following a hidden course.
Each ascent, a dance divine,
In the darkness, stars align.

With every breath, we claim our might,
Transforming heartbeats into flight.
Secrets whispered, dreams advance,
In the quiet, we find our chance.

Upward streams of hope and grace,
In this journey, find your place.
The secret path, a way to thrive,
In silent strength, we are alive.

Together, let our spirits soar,
Finding peace and so much more.
The ascendant light we seek to find,
In unity, our hearts entwined.

Unveiled Potential

In shadows deep, a spark ignites,
A whisper calls, the heart takes flight.
Dreams unfurl like petals wide,
Embracing change, we cast aside.

With every step, we dare to climb,
The mountain high, the test of time.
Beneath the weight, our spirits grow,
In unity, we'll face the flow.

Voices blend, a symphony,
Of hidden strengths now set to free.
In this moment, truth reveals,
The strength within, the light that heals.

Each heartbeat echoes, fierce and bold,
The stories vast, yet to be told.
With courage stitched in every seam,
We journey forth to chase the dream.

The path ahead may twist and bend,
Yet, in our hearts, the will won't end.
For every fear is but a guide,
To unveil what's hidden deep inside.

The Quiet Turning

In stillness soft, the world transforms,
A gentle breeze, a magic warms.
With open eyes, we start to see,
The quiet turning, meant to be.

Each moment still, a breath we take,
The heart feels soft, the will won't break.
As shadows fade, the dawn appears,
In silent grace, we shed our fears.

Footsteps echo on paths unknown,
In solitude, our strength has grown.
With every twist, a lesson learned,
In hidden places, we have yearned.

A whisper calls beneath the stars,
As destiny blueprints, near and far.
We trust the dance of time and space,
In quiet turning, find our place.

Let spirit guide through night's embrace,
In every pause, a sacred grace.
The journey leads, though silent now,
To vibrant life, we humbly bow.

Hushed Hopes

In shadows soft, where dreams reside,
A silent prayer, our hopes confide.
Whispers linger in the air,
As secret wishes drift with care.

Each moment's breath, a dancing spark,
In twilight glow, we find the arc.
With hearts alight, our visions soar,
Though hushed, they yearn for something more.

A flicker bright in darkest night,
Reminds us all to seek the light.
In stillness finds the loudest cry,
For hushed hopes never truly die.

Through every trial, in quiet grounds,
Resilience blooms where hope abounds.
In tender hands, we grasp the dream,
For every sigh, another theme.

As dawn will break the night's embrace,
We'll walk with courage, find our place.
In hushed hopes, our spirits sing,
Embracing all that life will bring.

Unseen Journeys

Beneath the stars, the paths unfold,
With every step, a tale retold.
In shadows cast, we roam unknown,
On unseen journeys, seeds are sown.

Each moment spent, a choice we make,
Through winding roads, our fears we shake.
With every stumble, wisdom gains,
In silent strength, the spirit reigns.

In realms unseen, our hearts do find,
The threads of fate intricately twined.
Through whispered dreams, we navigate,
Towards horizons that await.

A tapestry of time and space,
We walk the line, we find our grace.
In unseen journeys, trust the flow,
As life unveils what we must know.

With open hearts and minds set free,
We dance along this mystery.
In every pause, in every turn,
The fire within, forever burns.

Grace in the Quiet

In the stillness where shadows linger,
Gentle whispers brush the air.
A moment's pause, a tranquil finger,
Guides the heart, so free from care.

Beneath the stars, the night unfolds,
A tapestry of dreams untold.
In silence, grace softly enfolds,
As the world turns warm and cold.

Through tender breaths of softest night,
Hope unfurls its yearning wings.
In quiet hearts, there lies a light,
That in the darkness gently sings.

The rustle of leaves, the murmured breeze,
Echoes secrets of days gone by.
In the quiet, souls find ease,
And love blooms under the sky.

So sit awhile, let silence reign,
In quietude, our spirits soar.
In grace, we dance through joy and pain,
Finding peace forevermore.

The Whispered Path to Light

Amidst the fog where shadows creep,
A gentle voice calls from afar.
It beckons softly, as if to keep,
Our dreams beneath the morning star.

Footsteps tread on winding ways,
Where hope emerges from despair.
Each whispered promise gently stays,
Guiding hearts with steadfast care.

In every turn, a story weaves,
Through thickets thick with tangled fate.
The light above, the heart believes,
Emerging strong, we won't wait.

Through valleys deep, where sorrows lay,
A flicker warms the coldest night.
With every dawn, we find our way,
Step by step, we chase the light.

So walk with faith, let shadows part,
Embrace the warmth of morning's glow.
The whispered path, it calls the heart,
To trust in what the soul does know.

Muffled Strength

In the silence, courage grows,
Like roots that seek the depths of earth.
With every challenge, spirit flows,
A gentle strength that finds its worth.

Though storms may rage and tempests roar,
Inside the heart, a fire burns bright.
Through trials faced, we rise once more,
Finding power in the night.

A whispered hope in shadows cast,
Resilience swells with every breath.
In hidden battles, strength held fast,
A quiet force outlasts all death.

With every tear that paints the ground,
A seed of might breaks through the pain.
In muffled cries, a song is found,
A symphony that won't refrain.

So let the world be loud and bold,
As whispers turn to roars of might.
In every heart, a story told,
Of muffled strength that claims the light.

Hidden Heights of Hope

In valleys low, where shadows play,
A spark ignites beneath the stone.
Hidden heights, both bright and gray,
Whisper dreams of countless known.

Among the cliffs where eagles soar,
A promise lingers in the air.
Beyond the reach of evermore,
Hope finds a way for those who dare.

The mountains rise, a call to climb,
Through rugged paths we make our way.
In every step, we find the rhyme,
A melody that guides the day.

Through whispered winds and silent nights,
The stars above, they shine so clear.
In hidden heights, our spirit fights,
To chase away the veil of fear.

So, reach for dreams, let courage be,
Your guiding star, your inner guide.
With every breath, let hope be free,
In hidden heights, let hearts abide.

Silent Echoes of Greatness

In shadows cast by fleeting light,
Whispers of the past take flight.
They linger softly, yet they soar,
Greatness echoes evermore.

Time weaves tales in quiet tones,
Carved in stone, like ancient bones.
A glory wrapped in silence deep,
In every heart, these secrets keep.

The dreams of those who came before,
In whispered winds, they softly roar.
A tapestry of lives entwined,
In silent echoes, truth we'll find.

As night descends, the stars align,
Reflecting on the grand design.
Each moment holds a spark, a flash,
Of greatness lost, yet never past.

So let us honor those who dream,
Who dared to chase the rarest gleam.
In silent echoes, life shall sing,
As greatness blossoms, hearts take wing.

The Subtle Rise

In dawn's embrace, a whisper stirs,
A gentle shift, the silence blurs.
Colors blend in softest grace,
The subtle rise of a new place.

Golden rays break through the night,
As shadows dance in fading light.
Each heartbeat quickens with the day,
A tender touch lights up the way.

Mountains bow to the sun's warm glow,
In every crevice, life will grow.
The world awakes from dreams so deep,
In subtle rises, joy will leap.

A symphony of vibrant hues,
In every leaf, the morning dues.
A promise wrapped in morning's guise,
With every breath, we feel the rise.

So let us greet the day anew,
With open hearts, embrace the view.
For in each moment's soft surprise,
Awaits the magic of the rise.

Untold Stories in the Still

In silence waits a tale untold,
Where memories rest, both brave and bold.
The stillness breathes with every thought,
In quiet corners, dreams are caught.

A resting place for hearts that yearn,
In gentle sighs, the pages turn.
Each whisper calls from depths unseen,
A world alive, yet still and keen.

Through shadowed paths, the murmurs flow,
Stories hidden, waiting to show.
In every pause, the past will gleam,
Untold stories, life's sacred dream.

Time holds secrets in its embrace,
With every heartbeat, every trace.
In stillness found, we dare to seek,
Voices rise, when silence speaks.

So listen close and lend an ear,
For in the still, the truth is clear.
The echoes of our souls fulfill,
The untold stories in the still.

Paths of the Unseen

Beneath the surface, where shadows play,
Lie paths that twist and turn away.
In every step, a choice is found,
On roads of dreams, where hopes abound.

The hidden trails, they call our name,
With every path, we stake our claim.
In whispered tones, the journey starts,
Uniting souls and secret hearts.

Through tangled woods and winding streams,
We navigate the realm of dreams.
Though unseen, the trails connect,
With every turn, we learn, reflect.

In quiet moments, wisdom grows,
Through paths of life, the spirit flows.
The unseen guides us through the night,
Each hidden road leads to the light.

So take a breath, and trust the way,
Though paths may fade, we'll find our stay.
For in the unseen lies our fate,
The journey calls, it's never late.

The Softly Spoken Ascent

Whispers swirl in the gentle breeze,
Words of hope among the trees.
Each step taken, a quiet grace,
Hearts alight in a sacred space.

Dreams unfold in the morning light,
Guided softly through the night.
Step by step, the path revealed,
In the silence, souls are healed.

The stars above, like distant eyes,
Watching over as each heart flies.
With every breath, they soar and rise,
Through the clouds, beneath the skies.

A gentle hand leads the way,
In this brightening break of day.
Together we'll climb, side by side,
In this journey, we confide.

The softly spoken ascent calls,
Echoing through the ancient halls.
With courage found in tender hearts,
A new beginning as the old departs.

Barefoot on the Ladder of Dreams

Each rung brings a new-found thrill,
Barefoot steps with boundless will.
Dreams ascend, as shadows fade,
On this path our hopes are laid.

Skyward glances mixed with grace,
Climbing higher, we find our place.
With every breath, we touch the stars,
Floating gently, near and far.

Whispers of the night collide,
With morning's light, we turn the tide.
Barefoot souls on dreams we ride,
In this journey, we confide.

The ladder creaks with every climb,
Yet our spirits dance in rhyme.
Fingers stretch toward the unknown,
In this climb, we've truly grown.

So, chase the dreams that call your name,
On the ladder, play the game.
Step by step, we'll break the seams,
Forever barefoot in our dreams.

The Ascension of Shadows

Shadows stretch as daylight fades,
In the dusk where silence wades.
A dance begins in twilight's veil,
Where secrets whisper, soft and frail.

With every move, the night unfolds,
Tales of shadows, quietly told.
They blend and shimmer, rise and fall,
In this twilight, they enthrall.

Echoes linger in the air,
As stars awaken, bright and rare.
In their glow, shadows take flight,
Ascending high into the night.

Their forms like silk, they weave and play,
In the twilight, they sway and sway.
Invisible threads bind us tight,
In unity, beneath the light.

The ascension brings a mysterious charm,
Encasing dreams in a gentle arm.
Shadows rise, and we too shall,
Dance with echoes in their call.

The Secret Lift

An echo murmurs, soft and low,
In a hidden place, where secrets flow.
A door ajar, a world unseen,
The lift ascends, a space serene.

With every floor, a story grows,
Whispers shared where no one knows.
Climbing high in silent grace,
In this hidden, sacred space.

As the lift glides, time stands still,
Each moment wrapped in gentle thrill.
With hearts unbound, we rise and soar,
To places dreamed, forevermore.

The secret lift reveals our fate,
Where paths converge, and dreams await.
In unison, our hopes ignite,
As we ascend into the light.

Together we rise, side by side,
In this lift, our spirits glide.
With every rise, a new embrace,
In the secret lift, we find our place.

The Soft Surge of Change

Gentle waves on the shore,
Whisper tales of new dawns.
Each grain shifts with the breeze,
Hope dances in the light.

The moon guides the tides in flight,
While shadows softly blend.
Fleeting moments hold the truth,
Transformations intertwine.

A flower blooms in silence,
Petals wide with tender grace.
Nature's song of growing light,
Embracing shifts, we rise.

Beneath the calm facade,
A current flows unseen.
Life's gentle pulse breeds courage,
Emerging from the deep.

With every yearning heartbeat,
Change weaves through the air.
We ride the waves of fortune,
Guided by our dreams.

In the softest of moments,
We find the strength to soar.
Together, we'll embrace the dawn,
And welcome what's to come.

Subtle Currents of Progress

Ripples in a stream's flow,
Change takes time to reveal.
Each step echoes softly,
Building bridges of the heart.

Boundless journeys begin here,
In whispers of the night.
A spark ignites the courage,
Ready to unfurl wings.

Through shadows of the forest,
Truths emerge in the light.
Paths carved by gentle hands,
Lead us to the unseen.

With every breath we nurture,
The hope that feels like home.
A journey shared in silence,
Subtlety in our souls.

Waves of progress shape the shore,
A dance of give and take.
In the heart of the stillness,
We find strength to create.

And as we grow together,
We honor each small step.
With patience, we'll unravel,
The beauty that is change.

The Unheard Paradox

In shadows where we linger,
A truth begins to glow.
Silent doubts intertwine,
Lost yet found in the haze.

Voices soft as whispers,
Question all we perceive.
Hidden paths weave through silence,
Challenging our belief.

Hope resides in paradox,
What seems clear may not be.
Every answer births a question,
In the heart's depth we seek.

Amid the clamor of legends,
We harvest quiet dreams.
Unraveling threads of wisdom,
As we ponder the seams.

Fragments of our journey,
Scattered through the years.
Within the unexplained lies,
The courage to reveal.

With every breath we challenge,
The visions framed by doubt.
The unheard paradox unfolds,
In silence, we find strength.

Shadow-Laden Aspirations

Beneath the weight of shadows,
Aspire to break the chains.
Dreams flicker like candles,
Against the darkening sky.

Each step echoes softly,
On paths each heart must tread.
With courage as our armor,
We dance through quiet fears.

As twilight hangs above us,
Ambitions pulse like stars.
Guided by our visions,
We brave the night ahead.

In the stillness of the moment,
Voices whisper of hope.
Every heartbeat fuels the fire,
Igniting dreams anew.

Together we weave stories,
In the fabric of our souls.
Shadow-laden aspirations,
Illuminate the way.

So let us rise with purpose,
Emboldened by the night.
With every step, we conquer,
Defying what we fear.

Embracing the Stillness

In twilight's hush, the world slows down,
Whispers of thought weave through the air.
Nature cradles in a soft embrace,
Moments linger, free from despair.

The silent trees stand tall and proud,
Leaves rustle gently in the breeze.
A pause to breathe, to simply be,
Calming chaos, granting ease.

Stars begin their nightly dance,
While shadows deepen, quiet reigns.
In solitude, the heart finds peace,
And in stillness, love remains.

Reflections mirror the moonlit tide,
Soft glimmers of a fleeting dream.
Embracing what the night does hold,
Awakening from day's bright gleam.

Here in the silence, truths emerge,
With every heartbeat, we align.
In gentle nights, our spirits grow,
As stillness leads us to the divine.

Emergence from the Quiet

From depths of silence, flowers bloom,
A world reborn, fresh with delight.
Soft petals unfurl, colors bright,
Emerging softly from the night.

The dawn awakens soft and slow,
Birdsongs cradle the morning light.
Each note a promise of the day,
Emergence from the quiet night.

Through whispered winds, dreams take flight,
Every twinkle in the sky.
A journey starts in gentle hush,
As shadows fade and moments fly.

In stillness grows the heart's resolve,
To chase the echoes of the past.
Emerging from the quietude,
We find the strength that holds us fast.

With every breath, the courage grows,
To step from silence into sound.
From quiet roots, we rise anew,
Emerging from the peace we've found.

Wings Wrapped in Stillness

Beneath the calm, a hidden song,
As wings unfold in gentle grace.
In stillness lies a world alive,
Yearning for freedom, finding space.

With every breath, the tension fades,
Quiet moments knit the seams.
Wrapped in whispers, dreams take flight,
A canvas wrought with vibrant themes.

In solitude, the heart can soar,
Tracing paths of silent bliss.
Wings wrapped in stillness, poised to fly,
Embracing every heartfelt wish.

To lift above the noisy world,
In tranquility, peace alights.
With wings that flutter, soft and true,
Stillness nurtures new insights.

As dawn unfurls its golden brush,
We open wide, exploring deep.
In every stillness, new beginnings,
A promise held in silence's keep.

Silent Pulses of Potential

In quiet corners, dreams reside,
Silent pulses thrumming low.
Potential whispers like the breeze,
A sacred dance, a gentle flow.

Within the still, the heart can hear,
The echoes of what's yet to come.
Each breath a step toward the light,
A thrum of hope, a vibrant hum.

Through shadows cast by fleeting thoughts,
Quiet moments shimmer bright.
In silence, seeds begin to sprout,
Awakening within the night.

With every silence, strength is found,
To rise beyond the fears we know.
Silent pulses lead the way,
To futures filled with endless glow.

As night gives way to morning's song,
The pulse of dreams feels closer still.
In silent spaces, we attune,
To whispers of our boundless will.

Echoes of Untold Dreams

In the stillness of the night,
Whispers weave through silver beams.
Silent hopes take flight,
Carried softly by moonlit streams.

Stars hold secrets in their glow,
Each glimmer a gentle sigh.
Fleeting visions ebb and flow,
Painting futures in the sky.

Time stands still, yet moments flee,
Yet in shadows, dreams reside.
Unfolding like a mystery,
Where courage and heart abide.

Awake the whispers of the past,
Let echoes guide the way.
For dreams unchained will ever last,
In the cosmic dance of day.

Embrace the night, let it inspire,
As dawn unveils the light anew.
From ashes, rise with fervent fire,
To chase the dreams that once you knew.

The Quiet Surge

A gentle tide upon the shore,
Whispers of a coming wave.
Moments hold so much in store,
In silence, hearts begin to brave.

The world turns softly, yet it churns,
Beneath the calm, a force awakes.
Life's quiet murmurs twist and yearn,
As stillness cradles what it takes.

Beneath the surface, currents flow,
Unseen strings that pull and weave.
Echoes of all we cannot show,
A tapestry we dare believe.

Let patience blossom in the dark,
For strength emerges from the meek.
In shadows where our dreams embark,
The quiet surge begins to speak.

As dawn approaches, so does light,
Revealing paths once kept in shade.
With every breath, we claim our right,
To follow where the heart has strayed.

Unseen Wings of Dawn

In the hush before the day,
Colors whisper to the light.
Shadows fade, giving way,
To the warmth that ends the night.

Wings unseen, they grace the air,
Fluttering hopes on sunrise wings.
Carried forth without a care,
In the stillness, solace sings.

A canvas painted with the dew,
Nature's brush strokes find their place.
With each moment, skies renew,
The dawn reveals its gentle face.

In the promise of the morn,
Life awakens, softly bright.
From the depths where dreams are born,
Unseen wings take their flight.

So embrace the dawn's embrace,
And let it lift your soul to soar.
For in each golden, tender space,
The unseen wings will guide you more.

Shadows Ascending

In the twilight's gentle fold,
Shadows stretch and begin to rise.
Stories whispered, tales unfold,
Beneath the watchful, fading skies.

Moments drape in twilight's cloak,
Ghostly figures weave the night.
Echoes linger, softly spoke,
As shadows dance in waning light.

Each silhouette, a silent plea,
Carved in time, in hushed refrain.
Unraveled truths, come set us free,
Where each ascent brings joy and pain.

Breathe in deep the night's embrace,
Let shadows guide what's yet to be.
For within this darkened space,
Lie hopes that yearn to see the sea.

So rise with courage, let them lead,
These shadows hold the strength to climb.
Together, we will plant the seed,
Of dreams reborn in sacred rhyme.

The Stillness of Hope

In the quiet dawn's embrace,
Dreams awaken with a pace.
Whispers of a brighter day,
Chasing shadows far away.

Hearts beat softly, timing clear,
Casting away all doubt and fear.
In the hush, a promise glows,
Where the gentle river flows.

Stars still flicker in the night,
Guiding souls towards the light.
With each breath, we find our way,
Finding strength to face the day.

Through the storms that life may send,
Hope remains, our steadfast friend.
In the silence, courage found,
Resilience in every sound.

Together, we will rise and stand,
Weaving dreams with heart and hand.
In this stillness, hope will grow,
Harvesting the seeds we sew.

Veils of Serenity Lifting

Softly sacred whispers rise,
Veils of stillness kiss the skies.
Morning light begins to show,
As the shadows start to go.

Gentle breezes start to play,
Breathing life into the day.
Colors dance on petals bright,
Crafting art in golden light.

With each sigh, the world renews,
Painting life in vibrant hues.
Harmony begins to swell,
In the quiet, peace does dwell.

Nature's song in sweet refrain,
Lifting hearts from worry's chain.
In this moment, we will find,
Serenity that frees the mind.

Let us bask in joy's embrace,
Find our worth, our rightful place.
Veils of doubt now fall away,
Revealing hope in every ray.

Ghosts of Ambition

With every step, a shadow looms,
Echoes sing of unfulfilled blooms.
Whispers call from dreams once sown,
Ghosts of ambition, seeds we've grown.

In the mirror, faces stare back,
Chasing dreams on an unfinished track.
Every failure speaks a name,
Yet in struggle, sparks a flame.

Through the fog, a vision glows,
Paving paths where courage flows.
In each setback, lessons learned,
From the fires, our passion burned.

We'll rise above the haunting past,
Embracing change, we're built to last.
With every heartbeat, spirits soar,
Finding strength to seek much more.

Though the ghosts may dance and play,
We shall forge our own bright way.
Ambition calls, a vibrant spark,
Guiding us through the endless dark.

The Understated Journey

Stepping softly on this path,
Listening for the echoes' wrath.
Each moment, a gentle guide,
Carrying us, side by side.

Bridges built from love and pain,
Through the loss, we learn to gain.
In simplicity, beauty hides,
Flowing like the flowing tides.

Footprints left in softened ground,
Stories linger, wrapped around.
With each turn, a lesson learned,
In the quiet, passion burned.

Paths may twist, but hearts stay true,
In the stillness, find our cue.
Gratitude for every beat,
In this journey, life is sweet.

With the stars as our compass bright,
We will travel through the night.
Understated, yet so grand,
On this journey, hand in hand.

A Soft Rise to Somewhere

In the morning light, we rise,
Chasing dreams beneath clear skies.
Whispers of hope, the gentle breeze,
Life unfolds with quiet ease.

Across the fields, the flowers sway,
Guiding hearts along their way.
Each petal's dance, a silent cheer,
Reminding us that peace is near.

With every step, the world feels bright,
Nature's grace, a pure delight.
The path ahead holds promise sweet,
Where joy and solace gently meet.

Mountains loom, but we press on,
With every stumble, fears are gone.
Together we climb, shoulder to shoulder,
Finding strength as we grow bolder.

Atop the hill, we pause to see,
The endless sky, our destiny.
In the hush, the world stands still,
A soft rise to somewhere, by our will.

Cadence of the Heartbeat

In the quiet night, the heart knows,
A rhythm deep where presence flows.
Each pulse a whisper, soft and clear,
A melody only we can hear.

Footsteps echo, on paths unseen,
Threads of life weave in between.
With each thrum, a story unfolds,
Of love and loss, of dreams retold.

In the dance of time, we find our place,
Every moment, a fleeting grace.
The cadence sways like ocean tides,
Where hope and courage always bides.

Listen close, the heart will guide,
To places where our fears subside.
In the silence, truth reveals,
With each heartbeat, the soul heals.

Together we sway, a precious art,
In the cadence of the heartbeat, we start.
A song of life, forever spun,
In the rhythm, we become one.

Invisible Steps of Courage

In shadows cast by doubt and fear,
We take our steps, though none are near.
The path ahead, unclear and wide,
Yet in our hearts, we choose to stride.

Each movement whispers tales untold,
Of dreams protected, hearts of gold.
With silent strength, we forge ahead,
On invisible paths where angels tread.

Voices may falter, the night may loom,
Yet courage blooms amid the gloom.
For those who dare to rise and fight,
Invisible steps can spark the light.

With each brave choice, we stand and face,
The challenges that we embrace.
In unity, we build a bridge,
To cross the chasm, jump the ridge.

So take a breath, and feel the rise,
The fire within, beneath the skies.
Invisible steps, by faith we tread,
In courage found, our fears are shed.

Tranquil Ascent

As daylight breaks, the mountains call,
Inviting dreams to rise and fall.
In tranquil peace, we find our way,
Among the clouds that softly sway.

Each step we take, the world stands still,
Nature's breath, a soothing thrill.
Beneath the trees, the whispers flow,
Guiding hearts through sun and snow.

With every rise, a promise to keep,
Where secrets flourish, and shadows seep.
The path ahead, adorned with grace,
In tranquil ascent, we find our place.

Moments linger, wrapped in light,
As stars retreat, giving way to night.
In stillness, we breathe in the day,
And let our worries drift away.

So climb the heights, let spirits soar,
Where whispers echo forevermore.
In the tranquil ascent, dreams ignite,
Transforming the dark into radiant light.

Awakening Whispers

A gentle breeze stirs the night,
Soft breaths of hope take their flight.
Stars appear, and shadows fade,
In whispered dreams, new paths are laid.

Colors burst, the day is born,
In golden light, the heart is worn.
Echoes rise from earth so deep,
Awakening songs that life will keep.

Morning dew on petals gleam,
Nature sings a vibrant dream.
With every step, the spirit glows,
Through lush embrace where sunlight flows.

In stillness found in rustling leaves,
Resounding truths each moment weaves.
With every sigh, with every prayer,
Awakening whispers fill the air.

Quiet Ascension

In quiet moments, thoughts take flight,
Like birds that soar beyond the night.
The soul ascends on gentle streams,
In silence found, we chase our dreams.

Steps of grace on pathways worn,
In fading light, a new day's dawn.
With every heartbeat, stillness grows,
As nature's peace within us flows.

Mountains rise and valleys dance,
In every shadow, there's a chance.
With open hearts, we seek the truth,
In quiet ascension, we find our youth.

The morning brings a soft embrace,
In tranquil thoughts, we find our place.
As dreams intertwine with the divine,
We learn to breathe, to love, to shine.

Subtle Echoes

Softly ringing through the air,
Subtle echoes, sweet and rare.
Each whisper holds a tale unspun,
In quiet folds where hearts are one.

Shapes of darkness meld with light,
As dawn transforms the cloak of night.
Every journey, a rhythm flows,
In subtle echoes, truth bestows.

Gentle waves caress the shore,
In every tide, we seek for more.
With open ears, we hear the call,
In whispers shared, we'll never fall.

Through every path that winds and weaves,
The heart of nature softly breathes.
In moments pure, we come to know,
The power held in subtle flow.

The Unseen Climb

Beneath the veil, the spirit yearns,
In every lesson, wisdom turns.
An unseen climb beneath our feet,
To reach the heights where souls can greet.

With every step, the shadows fade,
In courage found, our fears are laid.
The mountain looms, yet we aspire,
With hearts ignited, fueled by fire.

Clouds may gather, storms may brew,
Yet strength awakens deep and true.
In struggles faced, we find our way,
The unseen climb reveals the day.

As horizons stretch, and spirits rise,
In unity, our voices fly.
The summit calls, our dreams unwind,
In every heart, a spark defined.

The Silent Triumph

In shadows deep where whispers lie,
A sturdy heart begins to fly.
With every step, the doubts must fade,
A silent strength, a bold crusade.

With each soft breath, the night obeys,
The dawn shall break, dispelling haze.
Though unacknowledged, the triumph's near,
In quiet moments, dreams appear.

The path unwinds with gentle grace,
Each stumble brings a warm embrace.
The light within begins to swell,
A silent story waits to tell.

As stars emerge, the fears dissolve,
In stillness, all the worlds revolve.
Though no applause shall mark the day,
A silent triumph finds its way.

And when the journey comes to close,
The heart shall wear its silent prose.
For in the shadows, light resides,
In silent triumph, hope abides.

Echoing Hopes

When whispers fade, in silence reign,
A heartbeat beats through joy and pain.
Each thought a spark within the dark,
Echoing hopes, a vital spark.

Across the fields where dreams take flight,
The seeds of change break through the night.
In every corner, light shall bend,
To weave the stories without end.

In trembling hands, they find their course,
With each whispered word, a steady force.
Together we rise, together we stand,
In echoing hopes, we take our hand.

Through every fear, through every tear,
The dreams we seek will soon be near.
For buried deep within the soul,
Echoing hopes, they make us whole.

With every dawn, new voices rise,
A chorus found beneath the skies.
In unity, the strength we find,
Echoing hopes, forever kind.

Stealthy Wings

In quiet nights, where shadows scurry,
The world moves on, no need to hurry.
With stealthy wings, the heart takes flight,
Embracing dawn and shunning night.

Through whispered dreams, our secrets soar,
Unseen by all, yet wanting more.
A gentle breeze, a hidden grace,
Stealthy wings in an unseen race.

In silent turns, the moments glide,
Where dreams reside and hopes abide.
With every beat, the rhythm grows,
On stealthy wings, the spirit flows.

Though shadows linger, fears may cling,
The heart will rise on stealthy wing.
With quiet strength, it know no bounds,
In whispered tones, adventure sounds.

When daylight breaks, the world will see,
The magic born of mystery.
For in the silence, wonders string,
On stealthy wings, we learn to sing.

Unheard Clarity

In bustling noise where minds collide,
Unheard clarity begins to guide.
A gentle flow that sweeps the soul,
In silent whispers, we feel whole.

Each fleeting thought, a quiet sign,
Amidst the chaos, stars align.
With steady breath, the fog recedes,
Unheard clarity plants its seeds.

As shadows pass, the truth unfolds,
In quiet moments, wisdom molds.
Through tangled paths, the journey shows,
In unheard clarity, the spirit grows.

With every choice, the heart will know,
In silence deep, our courage shows.
A beacon bright, where dreams are free,
Unheard clarity, our destiny.

So when the world feels loud and stark,
Seek the soft glow, ignite the spark.
For in the stillness, visions clear,
Unheard clarity draws us near.

Gentle Forces Unbound

Whispers of the morning light,
Awakening the softest sighs,
Nature's hand in tender flight,
Cleansing dreams where silence lies.

Rippling streams that dance and gleam,
Carries wishes on the breeze,
In every heart, a hidden dream,
Flowing softly through the trees.

Petals drop like feathered grace,
Landing softly on the ground,
In this still, embracing space,
Gentle forces swirl around.

Crickets chirp a lullaby,
Stars blink down a softened glow,
Nighttime sighs and dreams nearby,
In the dance of time's slow flow.

Together, we weave our paths,
Unbound by fate and time's decree,
In laughter's sweet, contagious wrath,
A world of love, forever free.

The Unvoiced Journey of the Soul

In shadows deep, a whisper calls,
A journey begun in silence,
Through hidden paths where darkness falls,
The soul seeks light with quiet defiance.

Each step taken is a heartbeat,
A rhythm felt, though words are few,
Footprints wash away in retreat,
Yet traces linger in the dew.

Mountains rise, both fierce and grand,
But valleys cradle tender dreams,
With nature's brush, the artist's hand,
Paints thoughts in moonlight's silver beams.

In solitude, wisdom whispers clear,
Guiding the heart along its way,
In every doubt, in every fear,
The unvoiced journey leads the day.

Reconnect with the essence pure,
Find strength in stillness, in the past,
The soul's embrace, forever sure,
In every breath, a truth amassed.

Shadows Feathering Upward

Feathers drift in twilight's hush,
Casting shadows soft and light,
They dance upon the evening's blush,
Weaving dreams into the night.

With every flutter, stories rise,
Whirling in the cool moonbeam,
Each shadow holds a thousand sighs,
A tapestry of whispered dreams.

Gentle hands of breeze unfold,
Curving softly through the trees,
As night's embrace begins to hold,
The world beneath, a hush of ease.

Stars ignite like scattered seeds,
Glistening jewels in endless dark,
A symphony of hidden needs,
Rising softly like a lark.

In shadows feathering upward high,
We find our truths within the night,
For every dream that dares to fly,
Is anchored deep in morning's light.

The Calm Before the Ascent

Silent whispers drape the air,
Calm before the surge of flight,
Hearts in stillness, unaware,
Of the storms concealed from sight.

Mountains loom, both fierce and high,
Yet in the peace, their shadows play,
Clouds collect like dreams in sky,
As hopes prepare to greet the day.

Each thought unsettled, gently pens,
A silent urge, a beckoning,
The moment pauses, then transcends,
Like breath held tight, awaiting spring.

The calm surrounds, a lull so pure,
Anticipation fills each heart,
A subtle pulse that will endure,
Before the journey's boldest start.

In this embrace of night and dawn,
We find the strength to aim and soar,
The calm before the dreams are drawn,
Releasing fears forevermore.

The Silent Pathway

In the hush of the morning light,
Footsteps tread, soft and light.
A trail where shadows dance slow,
Nature's secrets ebb and flow.

Trees arch high, their leaves embrace,
Ironbark heart, a tranquil space.
Whispers of wind weave through the air,
Silent stories linger there.

A path where doubts start to fade,
In every step, new dreams are laid.
With each breath, the world feels right,
Guided gently by the night.

As twilight falls, stars begin to shine,
A sign of hopes that intertwine.
The journey winds, yet feels so clear,
The silent pathway calls us near.

Whispered Transformations

In the shades of a morning glow,
Nature stirs, begins to flow.
Leaves shimmer in the golden light,
Awakening day from night.

The brook hums a gentle tune,
Reflecting the brightening moon.
Colors shift, evolve, and blend,
With each moment, change transcends.

Clouds meander, soft and white,
Carrying dreams of flight.
In their dance, life finds its way,
Transformations, come what may.

Whispers echo, softly spoken,
In the stillness, words unbroken.
Change is nature's sweetest art,
In every ending, a new start.

The Tranquil Uplift

Mountains rise, kissed by the sun,
A call to peace, a journey begun.
Breezes carry scents so sweet,
Nature's rhythm, a calming beat.

Among the pines, a secret space,
Where silence cultivates grace.
The call of the wild, gentle and pure,
In this haven, hearts find cure.

Birds take flight, low and free,
A symphony of serenity.
With every breath, tension unwinds,
In these moments, solace finds.

The evening sky begins to glow,
With hues of orange, pink, and low.
Wrapped in warmth, the day takes flight,
The tranquil uplift feels so right.

Beneath the Surface

In still waters, secrets hide,
Rippling depths where dreams abide.
Reflections of a world unseen,
Mysteries dwell where hearts convene.

Currents weave a tale untold,
Each drop, a treasure to behold.
Sinking deeper, fears dissolve,
In this realm, we start to evolve.

Glistening bubbles rise with glee,
Whispers of what we long to be.
Beneath the waves, hope is found,
In the silence, peace is profound.

A dance of shadows, light and dark,
Every ripple leaves its mark.
Exploring depths, we face the truth,
Beneath the surface, reclaim our youth.

The Murmurs of a New Dawn

Soft whispers brush the waking air,
Sunrise paints the world with care.
Birds take flight on gentle wings,
Embracing what the daylight brings.

Shadows dance as night retreats,
Hope ignites where heartbeats meet.
Every moment a fresh start,
Nature sings, uplifting hearts.

The dew-kissed grass, a silver sheen,
A canvas ripe, a vibrant scene.
Awake, arise, embrace the bliss,
A promise found in morning's kiss.

In this calm, the world takes breath,
Life begins anew from death.
Promises of joy unfurl,
In the dawn, our dreams swirl.

The horizon glows, a story spun,
With every rays, the battles won.
In silence, peace, a gentle chord,
The murmurs of the dawn restored.

Stillness Beckons

In the hush, where shadows play,
Time fades softly, drifts away.
Nature's grip holds the night tight,
Stars twinkle gently, fading light.

A single breath in the twilight,
Whispers linger, oh so slight.
Moonlight cloaks the quiet ground,
In stillness, solace can be found.

The trees stand tall, serene and grand,
Guardians of secrets, night's command.
Crickets sing a lullaby,
As the world exhales a sigh.

Gentle waves lap on the shore,
A rhythmic dance, forevermore.
Echoes of a tranquil grace,
Stillness beckons, time's embrace.

In this pause, we find our way,
Guided by the night's ballet.
A moment's peace, a fleeting chance,
In the quiet, souls can dance.

Unvoiced Triumphs

In silence, victories take their form,
Beyond the noise, the heart is warm.
Quiet battles fought and won,
Unseen glory, the journey spun.

The weight of dreams upon the chest,
Each step forward, an earnest quest.
Silent prayers on whispered lips,
Carried forth on faith's soft ships.

The thunder roars within the soul,
A quiet strength that makes us whole.
In the shadows, heroes rise,
Defying odds beneath the skies.

The world may not see the fight,
But in the dark blooms inner light.
Unvoiced triumphs, fierce and bright,
Fuel the spirit, guide our flight.

Moments cherished, tucked away,
Memories of a brighter day.
In the still, we learn to stand,
Unvoiced triumphs, hand in hand.

The Stealth of Serene Climb

Upward trails weave through the trees,
A gentle heart, the mind at ease.
Each footfall soft, no need for haste,
The view ahead, a breath to taste.

In quiet steps, the spirit thrives,
The mountain speaks, the journey drives.
With every rise, the world expands,
A tapestry woven by tender hands.

Whispers of wind brush against the skin,
Nature's grace, where dreams begin.
The summit glows, a tale unfolds,
In every heart, a story bold.

Through valleys low and peaks so high,
The path is carved under a vast sky.
With tranquil steps, the summit calls,
Serenity found as the spirit sprawls.

The stealth of climb, a dance so fine,
In every heartbeat, stars align.
Embracing heights where eagles soar,
In the whisper of peace, we seek more.

Soft Echoes of Resolve

In shadows deep, we find our way,
Through whispers soft, a light will stay.
The heartbeats strong, the pulse of fight,
Against the night, we'll seek the light.

Each step we take, we rise anew,
With every breath, resolve so true.
In quiet moments, strength we see,
A promise born, we'll always be.

Through storms that rage, we do not break,
With every challenge, paths we make.
In echoes faint, our courage grows,
Resilience blooms, in all it shows.

The road is long, yet we persist,
In dreams held close, we still resist.
With hands held tight, as shadows fade,
Together strong, we face the blade.

The echoes call, our spirits soar,
In unity, we will explore.
Through trials fierce, our hearts will sing,
In soft resolves, we find our wings.

Ascending Through The Mute

In silence thick, we learn to soar,
Beyond the words, there lies much more.
Through stillness deep, our voices rise,
In muted strains, we touch the skies.

Each moment spent, we build a bridge,
From quiet depths, we make the ridge.
With every pause, a space appears,
To breathe, to grow, to face our fears.

In shadows cast, we find the glow,
A whispered hope begins to flow.
With every challenge that we face,
We learn to move, we find our place.

The wind may howl, the world may scream,
Yet in the silent, we still dream.
An upward path, we start to climb,
Through stillness found, we sense the time.

As we ascend, the noise will fade,
In peaceful hearts, a choice is made.
Through softest sighs, we raise our eyes,
To meet the dawn, beneath the skies.

The Hushed Symphony of Growth

In gardens small, where stillness breathes,
Life opens wide, as nature weaves.
Each tender sprout, a story told,
In hushed tones of green and gold.

The soil rich, with care it feeds,
From quiet roots, a hope proceeds.
With every raindrop, dreams take flight,
In secret hours, we see the light.

Yet storms will come, they test our might,
Through raging winds, we hold on tight.
For in the dark, we learn to stand,
With open hearts, we'll understand.

In every pause, a lesson waits,
The hush of life, it cultivates.
Through whispers soft, we break the mold,
And nurture strength, as stories unfold.

A symphony born in silence sweet,
In every note, a heart will beat.
Together we rise, through highs and lows,
In hushed harmony, our spirit grows.

Unheard Resurgence

In echoes lost, we rise again,
From ashes deep, we claim our zen.
Through trials faced, we stand up tall,
In unheard strength, we heed the call.

The silent winds, they weave a tale,
Of whispered hope, beyond the pale.
Resurgence blooms in quiet night,
In shadows cast, we find our light.

With every heartbeat, fate we mold,
In muted strength, our truth unfolds.
Through darkest times, we'll find a way,
For in the hush, we learn to stay.

The world may spin, yet we'll remain,
In strength renewed, we break the chain.
With silent cries, we'll rise and soar,
Through unheard dreams, we find much more.

In every breath, the past we shed,
Towards brighter skies, we boldly tread.
A journey shared, through thick and thin,
In unheard resurgence, we begin.

Shadows of Growth

In silence, roots do weave,
Beneath the soil, they cleave.
Each whisper of the breeze,
Nurtures dreams on bended knees.

The sun peeks through the trees,
Casting warmth, a gentle tease.
Leaves unfurl with tender grace,
Embracing light, a new embrace.

Each shadow tells a tale,
Of journeys worn, yet bold and frail.
In every crack, a secret blooms,
Carving paths through endless glooms.

Seasons weave a vibrant thread,
While fragile visions gently spread.
With patience, growth begins anew,
From subtle shades, bright colors flew.

So heed the dance of night and day,
In every pause, the heart will sway.
For growth is found in twilight's grace,
An endless path, our sacred space.

Invisible Eminence

In shadows cast, they stand so still,
With quiet strength, they bend to will.
Unseen forces shape the tide,
Invisible, yet full of pride.

Each gentle push, a silent plea,
Creates a shift, a symphony.
As whispers churn, the world awakes,
A dance of fate, the heart it breaks.

In every heartbeat, they reside,
The feelings deep that cannot hide.
A power felt, but rarely seen,
In every space, they weave between.

The tapestry of dreams unfolds,
In threads of gold, the truth retold.
In hidden realms, they find their place,
Connecting souls with unseen grace.

So honor all that lies beneath,
The life that breathes with every wreath.
For invisible, yet oh so vast,
It's in their depths, our shadows cast.

The Soft Surge

Like whispers brushed on gentle winds,
A soft surge, where life begins.
In quiet pools, reflections gleam,
As hopes ebb forth, a tender dream.

With each wave, the heart responds,
To soft beats of timeless bonds.
In open spaces, sighs collide,
While nature's art, it will confide.

The murmurs blend, both near and far,
As moonlit paths become a scar.
A surge of colors, wild and free,
In harmony, we learn to be.

Each droplet dances, float or sink,
In waters deep, we pause to think.
The rhythm flows, a soothing sound,
In every wave, new hope is found.

So feel the surge, let go of fear,
Allow the soft to draw you near.
For beauty thrives in gentle sway,
In every dawn, we find our way.

Serene Awakening

In dawn's embrace, the world unfolds,
With hues of pink and whispers bold.
In quiet morn, the heart takes flight,
As dreams dissolve in warming light.

The dew-kissed grass, a jeweled crown,
Beneath the sky, a soft renown.
Each breath a gift, a tender sway,
In nature's arms, we'll gently play.

With every step, the earth will sigh,
As birds begin their morning cry.
A melody of life appears,
Erasing shadows, calming fears.

Awake, we rise, both strong and free,
Embracing all that's yet to be.
In every moment, wisdom flows,
A serene path, the heart bestows.

So linger here, let worries fade,
In peaceful thoughts, our souls are laid.
For every day, a gift we take,
In serene light, we surely wake.

Hushed Elevation

In the quiet crest of dawn,
Soft whispers greet the light.
Clouds drape like a gentle shawl,
Embracing day from night.

Mountains stand in silent grace,
Guardians of the morn.
A breeze carries secrets old,
In a world reborn.

Birds take flight on unseen wings,
Dancing with the sun.
Every heartbeat syncs in time,
With the earth's soft hum.

In this tranquil, high expanse,
All worries fade away.
Hearts float on a quiet sigh,
As thoughts begin to play.

In hushed elevation's glow,
We find our spirit soar.
With every breath, a promise made,
To seek and to explore.

Gentle Revolt

In the shadows, whispers rise,
A wave of hearts unite.
Gentle hands can shift the tides,
Bringing forth the light.

Eyes that shine with steadfast hope,
Break the chains of doubt.
Together we will forge new paths,
A future forged, no rout.

With each step, a heartbeat strong,
Marching hand in hand.
Resilient in our silent roar,
We change this stubborn land.

Roots break through the hardened ground,
As flowers start to bloom.
Life awakens in revolt,
Dispelling all the gloom.

In gentle fervor, we arise,
With dreams we won't dismiss.
The world anew begins to turn,
In unity, we persist.

Stillness in Motion

In the dance of swaying trees,
Time stands still yet flows.
A breeze carries thoughts away,
Where only silence knows.

Ripples trace the water's skin,
As shadows shift and glide.
The world spins on its axis,
While moments softly bide.

Yet in each fleeting heartbeat,
A universe awakes.
In stillness, we find the pulse,
Of every choice we make.

Footfalls echo in the dusk,
Minds in quiet chase.
The world unveils her secrets,
In this gentle embrace.

Motion whispers of the past,
Stillness cradles the now.
Together they weave a tapestry,
In life's eternal vow.

Soaring Shadows

Beneath the arch of twilight skies,
Dark shapes begin to dance.
A tapestry of whispered dreams,
In shadows they entrance.

Wings that glide on evening's breath,
Trace paths of silent flight.
In the hush of fading light,
They claim the coming night.

Echoes of forgotten tales
Drift softly through the air.
Soaring shadows of the past,
Bring stories rich and rare.

The moon casts silver on the ground,
As fears begin to fade.
In the calm between the beats,
Courage finds its shade.

So let the shadows hold us close,
As we embrace the night.
For in the dark, we find our wings,
To soar beyond the light.

The Unseen Climb of Hope

In shadows deep where dreams reside,
The whispers of a heart collide.
Through valleys low and mountains high,
A glimmer shines, it won't say die.

Each step we take, though rough the road,
Our spirits lift, a heavy load.
In every trial, we start anew,
The unseen climb, our strength breaks through.

With every heartbeat, courage grows,
Through stormy nights, resilience shows.
Though paths are hidden from our gaze,
We carry forth in endless ways.

In quiet moments, hope ignites,
A spark of joy in darkest nights.
We rise again, we can't be stopped,
For in our hearts, the seed is dropped.

The journey long, the end unclear,
Yet love and faith will always steer.
So onward bound, we chase the light,
The unseen climb, a hopeful sight.

Beneath the Surface

In stillness deep, the secrets swirl,
The world above, a distant pearl.
Beneath the waves, where shadows play,
The heartbeats echo, dreams on sway.

Unseen connections start to weave,
In darkened depths, we dare believe.
What lies below, a treasure find,
A dance of thought, a tide unkind.

Each ripple sings a silent song,
Of life and loss, where we belong.
From depths of sorrow, springs arise,
The hidden truths, we seek in skies.

So dive with me, let's lose the fears,
In ocean's cradle, dry our tears.
For what is found beneath the wave,
Is worth the plunge, it's hope we save.

In gentle swells, our spirits glide,
Beneath the surface, love won't hide.
A world unseen, we boldly tread,
In longing hearts, new paths are bred.

Rising

The dawn appears with gentle grace,
A golden hue paints every face.
From slumber wakes the silent night,
With whispers soft, the day ignites.

We stand and stretch, embrace the sun,
For every end, a race begun.
The roots we plant in fertile ground,
With each new morn, our hopes rebound.

Through trials faced and shadows cast,
We gather strength from all that's past.
With every heartbeat, dreams take flight,
In glorious hues, we find the light.

So let the winds of change now blow,
In vibrant paths, our spirits grow.
Together we will rise anew,
With every dawn, life's canvas blue.

In unity, our voices soar,
With courage held, together, more.
With open hearts, in unison,
We rise as one, our journey won.

Gentle Uprising

A subtle swell, the whispers call,
In quiet strength, we rise, yet small.
With tender hands, we forge the way,
A gentle tide, we won't dismay.

The world may seem a heavy cloak,
But in our hearts, a fire stokes.
Determined souls, we gather round,
In gentle uprising, truth is found.

We lift each other, one by one,
In every shadow, hope begun.
The seeds of change we sow with care,
A softer path, a love laid bare.

With every voice, a symphony,
In harmony, we sing to be.
No loud crusade, but steady hands,
In gentle hearts, the power stands.

Let kindness flow, a river wide,
In unity, we will abide.
For in our wills, the strength resides,
In gentle ways, the world Collins.

The Hidden Spring

In secret glades, where shadows dance,
A hidden spring, a fleeting chance.
From stones of time, the waters flow,
A source of life, where echoes grow.

Each drop a whisper, soft and clear,
Tells tales of love that conquer fear.
In nature's arms, our hearts align,
We find the warmth, in worlds divine.

Beneath the boughs, the essence flows,
Where every wound, the water knows.
A soothing balm for weary souls,
In hidden springs, our spirit rolls.

When thirst is quenched, the journey's bright,
The shadows fade; we welcome light.
From depths within, the strength will rise,
A hidden spring, where hope complies.

So seek these springs, both near and wide,
In every heart, let love abide.
For in the stillness, life renews,
The hidden spring, our truth imbues.

The Boundary of Silence and Flight

In the hush of dusk, dreams take wing,
Echoes linger, softly they sing.
Between the stars, whispers glide,
A silent promise where hopes abide.

Moonlight dances on the edge of night,
Casting shadows in gentle flight.
Beyond the veil where silence grows,
A tapestry of quiet flows.

Wings stretched wide, a heart set free,
In the stillness, the soul can see.
The boundary drawn in twilight's grace,
A hidden journey, a sacred place.

Softly weaving through absence and space,
A tender search for the lost embrace.
With every breath, the silence calls,
In the vastness, the spirit sprawls.

In whispered tones, the night confides,
A thousand stories where magic hides.
As time unwinds, the whispers twine,
In the boundary of silence, we intertwine.

Silken Ascent in Shadow

Climbing high where shadows weave,
A silken thread the heart believes.
In the quiet, courage blooms,
As light retreats, the darkness looms.

Every step cloaked in soft embrace,
The spine of night, a tranquil space.
With silent grace, we rise and tread,
In the fabric of whispers, we are led.

Through veils of dusk, we find our way,
Upon the brink of night and day.
Each breath a vow, each glance a spark,
As we ascend from light to dark.

In sheltered depths, our spirits soar,
Finding strength in shadows' lore.
The silken ascent, our journey's cry,
To touch the stars hidden on high.

Embracing night in clusters bright,
Illuminating the path with light.
Together we rise, hand in hand,
In the silken shadows, we understand.

The Subdued Climb

In morning mist where echoes fade,
A journey starts with hope displayed.
Each step a whisper, softly tread,
In the quiet, dreams are fed.

The path is steep, the air is thin,
With strength within, we choose to begin.
Through trials faced, we rise above,
In muted tones, we find our love.

Nature cradles as we ascend,
A solemn promise, a steadfast friend.
In every breath, resilience glows,
Through the struggle, our spirit grows.

With shadows falling, we'll not despair,
In the muted light, we find our share.
The subdued climb, a sacred grace,
Where every challenge learns its place.

Together we forge through silence and strife,
Chasing echoes that pulse with life.
Onward we tread, our hearts aligned,
In the subdued climb, we are defined.

The Quiet Inheritance

In softest whispers, legacies lie,
Tales of love that never die.
A gentle touch, a knowing glance,
The quiet inheritance of chance.

Time's tender thread weaves through our veins,
Holding stories of joys and pains.
In silence shared, the past entwines,
Embracing moments in sacred signs.

Inheritance not of gold or fame,
But the warmth of hearts that call our name.
Each breath a memory, each laugh a gift,
In quiet inheritance, spirits lift.

Pages turned in the book of souls,
Showing us where true wealth unfolds.
In bonds forged deep through love's embrace,
The quiet inheritance finds its place.

Guided by the echoes of those before,
We gather strength to seek and soar.
In the stillness, we find our way,
The quiet inheritance of yesterday.

Climbing Beyond the Silent Veil

Through misty paths we slowly tread,
The world below, like whispers, fled.
Each step a heartbeat, soft and clear,
We journey on, dispelling fear.

The summit waits with arms aglow,
A promise held in flakes of snow.
As shadows dance against the light,
We seek the dawn, embrace the night.

Upon the heights, the silence sings,
Beyond the bounds of earthly things.
In ethereal realms, spirits roam,
We find our truth, we find our home.

The winds of change begin to stir,
With every climb, we're bound to blur.
A tapestry of dreams unspooled,
In heights of hope, we are renewed.

With laughter echoing through the skies,
We rise, we fall, but never die.
The journey shapes us, raw and real,
In secret breaths, we make our deal.

Gaining Ground in Solitude

In quiet nooks where shadows play,
I find my thoughts, my heart's ballet.
The world outside may rush and race,
But in this stillness, I find grace.

Each moment stretches, time withdraws,
With gentle hands, I pause, I draw.
Embracing whispers of the night,
In solitude, I seek the light.

The echo of my breath resounds,
In silence deep, my spirit bounds.
While nature wraps me in her arms,
I trust her ways, her ancient charms.

With every glance, the heart can know,
The seeds of wisdom start to grow.
In quiet strength, I make my stand,
Gaining ground, the world at hand.

Alone but never lonely here,
In shadows bright, I conquer fear.
With every stir, the soul ignites,
In solitude, I reach new heights.

The Hidden Climb

Beneath the surface, trails unseen,
A journey waits, serene yet keen.
With every twist, the path reveals,
The strength within, the heart that heals.

In whispering winds, I find my call,
Each challenge faced, I rise, I fall.
The mountain's heart, a secret sung,
In hidden climbs, my soul is strung.

Through tangled trees and winding stone,
I unearth places I have grown.
The summit's grace, a fleeting dream,
In each ascent, I learn to beam.

The echoes of my past, they fade,
With every step, new bonds are made.
In nature's breath, the spirit's light,
The hidden climb reveals the fight.

As dawn meets dusk, horizons bend,
The fearless heart begins to mend.
In every hidden surge of pride,
I reach for love, I reach for sky.

A Symphony of Quietude

In a realm where silence reigns,
The heart beats soft, the spirit gains.
Melodies of stillness weave,
A symphony, we dare believe.

With every pause, a note takes flight,
In twilight's grasp, day meets the night.
The whispers of the wind align,
In quietude, we intertwine.

Each rustle, sigh, the world unfolds,
In gentle hues, serenity molds.
Harmony in nature's breath,
In silent spaces, life finds depth.

From mountain tops to valleys low,
The silent song begins to flow.
In stillness, count the stars above,
A quiet symphony of love.

As time stands still, the heart will soar,
With every beat, we yearn for more.
In quietude, our dreams align,
A symphony of worlds divine.

The Mysterious Lift

In a corner stands a door,
Whispers of tales from the floor.
Rusty hinges softly sigh,
What awaits when you step nigh?

Shadows dance in flickering light,
Drawn to the pull of curious flight.
Upward lifts the heart and mind,
In this lift, what will we find?

Faces fade, as the world grows small,
Each ascent feels like a call.
Into the unknown we drift and sway,
Where mysteries weave and play.

Time holds breath, suspended high,
As dreams and fears begin to fly.
The lift ascends to realms untold,
In silence, we gain courage bold.

With a jolt, stops its rise,
What lies beyond, a sweet surprise?
Gather strength and take the chance,
Unlock the door—embrace the dance.

Dreams Daring to Soar

Underneath the moonlit sky,
Whispers of hopes begin to fly.
Each star twinkles, bright and bold,
A canvas where dreams unfold.

Hearts beat loud in silent prayer,
For wings to lift us from despair.
Golden chances drifting near,
Dare to dream without fear.

Through valleys deep and mountains high,
We chase the sun as it climbs by.
Boundless skies call our name,
In this journey, we stake our claim.

With every step, our spirit grows,
Embracing paths that nature chose.
Adventure waits with open arms,
Where courage meets its countless charms.

So take a leap, let shadows fade,
In flight or fall, be not dismayed.
For dreams that dare to take their wings,
Bring to life the brightest things.

Unspoken Horizons

Beneath the surface, secrets hide,
Unseen paths where dreams reside.
Silence speaks in quiet tones,
Guiding hearts like restless stones.

Eyes are drawn to distant shores,
Where endless skies meet open doors.
Whispers weave through tangled trees,
Bringing forth the gentle breeze.

Time unravels, softly flows,
This journey is where courage grows.
Each step holds a tale unheard,
In the spaces between the words.

Horizon waits, a painter's brush,
In colors bold, a vibrant hush.
With every dawn, we seek to find,
The wisdom of the heart, the mind.

Let us wander through the gray,
Embrace the light that leads the way.
Unspoken dreams rise like the dawn,
In every heart, there's magic drawn.

Mighty Muted Movements

In the quiet, forces flow,
Softly pushing, gently grow.
The weight of worlds, yet still unseen,
In the shadows, we glean what's been.

Branches sway with whispered might,
Roots entwine beneath the night.
Silent strength in every grain,
Nature's pulse in calm refrain.

Gentle ripples across a lake,
Echoes of decisions made.
In stillness, freedom finds a way,
To dance along the soft delay.

Awakened hearts of those who listen,
In hushed reverence, spirits glisten.
Though movements may feel slow and small,
Each heartbeat tells us, we can stand tall.

From muted whispers, stories rise,
The unseen forces, the quiet skies.
With every breath, let's find the sway,
For thunder waits in the light of day.

The Subdued Climb

With each step, the silence grows,
The path leads where the soft wind blows.
Whispers of the trees surround,
In this peace, my heart is found.

The shadows dance on ancient stone,
Guiding me to places unknown.
Each breath a sigh, each thought a prayer,
In this stillness, I lay bare.

The higher I rise, the lighter I feel,
Softening edges, the world's appeal.
A muted echo of dreams in tow,
In twilight's embrace, I softly go.

The summit awaits, quiet and clear,
A moment of truth, no trace of fear.
Nature sings a gentle hymn,
In this haven, my soul can swim.

A journey made of tranquil grace,
With every crest, I find my place.
In the subdued climb, I find my light,
Guided by stars through the deepening night.

Muted Revelations

In the stillness of dawn's first glow,
Secrets whisper, soft and slow.
Nature's language speaks so clear,
In muted tones, I draw near.

Leaves rustle with tales untold,
Fables woven, rich and bold.
The world unveils its soft disguise,
In silence, truth begins to rise.

Eyes closed tight, I breathe it in,
Life's wisdom where dreams begin.
Each moment filled with quiet grace,
In muted revelations, I find my place.

The air is thick with thoughts profound,
Lost and found, we're all unbound.
Revelations that come and go,
In the hush, our spirits flow.

As shadows lengthen, I sit and wait,
Each heartbeat a thread that we create.
In this gentle fold of time,
The muted truth feels so sublime.

Gentle Awakening

Morning breaks with a tender sigh,
Sunlight spills from the azure sky.
Birds begin their cheerful call,
In gentle waking, I feel it all.

Soft rays touch the earth with grace,
Nature's rhythm in a sweet embrace.
Each petal opens, dew drops gleam,
In this moment, I dare to dream.

The world awakens, slow and sweet,
With the dance of shadows at my feet.
I take a step into the day,
In gentle waking, I find my way.

Moments linger, time feels kind,
With open heart, my soul aligned.
In the stillness, I welcome light,
As day unfolds, so pure and bright.

Beneath the sky, my spirit soars,
In gentle whispers, my heart explores.
This waking world, a canvas wide,
In the tender morning, I'll abide.

Soothing Ascendancy

Beneath the clouds, a quiet reign,
Mountains whisper as they restrain.
In the shadows, a calm prevails,
Soothing currents in hidden trails.

The journey upward, soft and slow,
With every step, the spirit grows.
Nature's cradle holds me near,
In soothing ascendance, I shed my fear.

The air is crisp, the path divine,
In silence, I seek the sign.
Glimmers of light through forest veins,
In this embrace, my heart remains.

Every breath, a gentle kiss,
Heightened senses filled with bliss.
With the dawn, I rise anew,
In soothing ascendance, I break through.

The summit glows, a realm of peace,
A tranquil heart, my soul's release.
Here in stillness, life and breath,
Soothing ascendance, beyond death.

The Serene Pinnacle

Atop the peak, the sky unfolds,
A quiet hush, a tale retold.
Nature's canvas, pure and vast,
In gentle breezes, shadows cast.

The sun dips low, a golden hue,
Mountains watch with wisdom true.
Footsteps traced in gravel's grip,
In stillness, dreams begin to slip.

Clouds drift by, like thoughts in flight,
Pausing moments, calm and light.
Here, time ticks at a softer pace,
In this embrace, I find my place.

Stars awaken, a shimmering sea,
Whispers of night call out to me.
With every breath, the world feels right,
Atop the pinnacle, bathed in light.

A serene promise through the years,
Holding close both joy and fears.
In nature's arms, we rise and fall,
At the pinnacle, we find it all.

Silenced Aspirations

In shadows deep, the dreams lay still,
Veiled whispers, unspoken will.
Plans abandoned, paths untrod,
Faint echoes of what once was.

Each morning brings a muted sigh,
A canvas blank, beneath the sky.
Hope flickers like a fading star,
Distance grows, the journey far.

The heartbeats fade in crowded rooms,
Buried beneath the weight of gloom.
Voices drowned by doubt's decree,
Longing for what was meant to be.

Yet in the stillness, sparks ignite,
A feeble glow, a flicker of light.
The courage to chase dreams anew,
Awakens softly, breaking through.

Though silenced dreams may bear their scars,
They pulse with rich and hidden wars.
A chorus stirs, the silence breaks,
In every heart, a heartbeat wakes.

Growth in Stillness

In quiet moments, seeds take root,
Beneath the soil, a muted shoot.
Time drips slowly like morning dew,
Awakening the world anew.

Branches stretch in whispered grace,
Finding strength in the slow embrace.
Gentle winds, they sway and bend,
Resilience blooms, and fears transcend.

Patience whispers in the night,
Every star holds dreams in sight.
Soil enriched by trials faced,
In calm, our spirits find their place.

Through seasons' change, we learn to see,
That real growth comes quietly.
Roots plunge deep, yet reach for skies,
In stillness, our true spirit flies.

So cherish moments, small yet grand,
In the still, we make our stand.
For every leaf that greets the day,
Is growth in stillness, come what may.

Whispers of Ascent

In twilight's glow, we start to rise,
Embracing dreams, we touch the skies.
Steps that linger on ancient stone,
Echo the paths we call our own.

Winds of change, a soft caress,
In every breath, we find our quest.
Chasing shadows, the spirits dance,
Within the silence, we take a chance.

With every climb, the heart ignites,
A journey's strength, a world of sights.
Mountains loom, yet hope remains,
In whispers soft, our essence gains.

The stars align, a guiding touch,
Each single step means so much.
Through valleys low and peaks so tall,
We rise together, we won't fall.

As dawn unfolds, the dream persists,
In whispered hopes, our souls exist.
Together in this vast expanse,
We find our voices, hear our dance.

Veils of Dawn

Veils of soft light break the night,
Shadows retreat from the sight.
Whispers of warmth gently tease,
Awakening nature with ease.

Birds begin to serenade,
In the crisp air, dreams cascade.
Colors bloom as moments pause,
Life unfolds with silent applause.

Morning dew on blades of grass,
Reflects the sun's golden mass.
A promise of joy in each ray,
Inviting the world to play.

As the horizon starts to glow,
Hope ignites with a gentle flow.
Veils of dawn embrace the day,
In nature's rhythm, we sway.

Each heartbeat echoes, pure and free,
In harmony with all we see.
Veils of dawn, a sacred view,
Reminding us of life anew.

Whispered Uprising

Among the shadows, voices rise,
Soft as the wind beneath the skies.
Dreams intertwined with silent thought,
In every heart, a spark is caught.

Fragments of hope in gentle streams,
Stirring the world, igniting dreams.
Whispers of change fill the air,
Awakening souls, raw and bare.

A rhythm of courage starts to beat,
In unity, we find our feet.
Together we stand, hearts ablaze,
In the glow of a brand-new phase.

Hands held high, we rise as one,
Chasing shadows, embracing the sun.
Whispers turn to a mighty roar,
An uprising born from the core.

With every step, we forge the way,
Towards a brighter, bolder day.
Whispered uprising, a song of peace,
In the dawn of love, we find release.

Muffled Flourish

In a world where silence reigns,
Whispers hide in soft terrains.
Muffled sounds echo the past,
Yearning for dreams that hold steadfast.

Petals fall, adorned with grace,
Nature's art, a quiet embrace.
Colors blend in muted streams,
Muffled flourish of fading dreams.

Gentle sways in evening light,
Brush of shadows, soft twilight.
Moments linger, yet slip away,
In the hush where memories stay.

Yet in this silence, hope can bloom,
In hidden corners, life's perfume.
Muffled flourish, a daring spark,
While shadows dance in the dark.

Listen close, to what is not said,
In the stillness, we are led.
Muffled worlds in our hearts reside,
Whispers of joy that cannot hide.

Tranquil Ascent

Gently we climb, with hearts aligned,
Every step, a path designed.
In the quiet, we find our grace,
A tranquil ascent to a sacred space.

Nature's breath guides our way,
Under the vast sky, we sway.
Mountains rise, holding the sky,
Inviting us to reach up high.

Whispers of breeze, soft and clear,
Carrying dreams that draw us near.
With every turn, the view expands,
Life unfolds in gentle hands.

Sunset glows, painting the dusk,
In the air, a sweet dusk musk.
Tranquil moments fill the soul,
In stillness, we begin to whole.

As night descends, stars ignite,
In the vastness, we find light.
Tranquil ascent, a journey true,
To the rhythm of me and you.

Pathways of Serenity

In gentle whispers, the breezes flow,
Through verdant forests, where soft lights glow.
Each step a journey, calm and slow,
Beneath the sky, where dreams bestow.

Winding rivers play a tranquil tune,
Reflections dance beneath the moon.
Nature's cradle, a sacred rune,
Guiding hearts to sweet monsoon.

Meadows stretch in hues of gold,
With stories of the brave and bold.
In peaceful arms, our fears unfold,
With tranquil sights, life's tale is told.

Amongst the trees, a silence sings,
Echoing softly, the hope it brings.
In solitude, the heart takes wings,
As wisdom flows from nature's springs.

In every moment, find your space,
Where love and light embrace each place.
On pathways worn, we find our grace,
In serenity's warm embrace.

Unvoiced Horizons

Beyond the veil where shadows play,
Lies a horizon, lost in gray.
With silent dreams that drift away,
In whispers soft, they gently sway.

Unseen journeys, each step we take,
In twilight's glow, the stillness wakes.
In quiet moments, heartache breaks,
While solitude in silence aches.

Stars above in velvet night,
Hidden glimmers, a distant sight.
With unvoiced hopes, we seek the light,
In silent dawn, we find our flight.

Beneath the weight of untold fears,
Echoes linger, muffled tears.
Yet through the pain, love reappears,
In soft embraces, drawing near.

On paths we tread, no sound is heard,
Yet in our hearts, we feel the stirred.
In unvoiced dreams, our souls conferred,
Through quiet nights, our spirits spurred.

Unnoticed Blossoming

In corners where the shadows dwell,
Soft petals bloom, a secret spell.
In muted tones, they shyly swell,
Their beauty lost, a tale to tell.

Yet in the dawn, they stretch and reach,
Through whispered winds, their lessons teach.
In every bud, life's truths they preach,
Unnoticed grace, within each breach.

Among the cracks where silence reigns,
Colorful heartbeats break the chains.
With gentle strength, love's light remains,
In quiet hearts, where hope sustains.

The world may rush, forget the rare,
But in their presence, dreams lay bare.
In humble beauty, they declare,
Life's fragile wonders everywhere.

So pause a while, and take a glance,
At unnoticed blooms that sweetly dance.
In small delights, hearts find their chance,
To embrace life in a quiet trance.

Quietude's Rise

With morning light, the world awakes,
In whispered calm, the silence breaks.
A gentle hush, the heart remakes,
As quietude in stillness takes.

As nature breathes in softest sighs,
From dawn to dusk, the spirit flies.
In tender glances, peace complies,
In moments still, the soul complies.

Beneath the vast and endless skies,
The beauty of the moment lies.
In every breath, the heart replies,
To quietude, where wisdom lies.

Where chaos fades and troubles cease,
In silence found, a hidden peace.
With every step, our burdens lease,
In quietude, our hearts increase.

So let us find that still embrace,
In every journey, every place.
For in the calm, we find our grace,
In quietude, our fears erase.

The Hidden Height

Amidst the trees, a secret path,
Where sunlight dances, shadows laugh.
A journey calls, my heart takes flight,
To find the peak, the hidden height.

With every step, the world unfolds,
A tapestry of green and gold.
Mountains loom, majestic, bright,
Whispering tales of day and night.

The air grows thin, a breath of peace,
A gentle sigh, my thoughts release.
I climb with hope, my spirit light,
To touch the sky, this hidden height.

The stars emerge, a glittering guide,
In quiet awe, I stand beside.
The night reveals a world so wide,
In the embrace of cosmic tide.

I stand amazed, as dreams take wing,
On mountain tops, the heart will sing.
Forever drawn to nature's might,
In search of love, the hidden height.

Whispers of Morning

Softly breaks the dawn's embrace,
The sun awakens, paints the space.
Birds begin their sweet refrain,
A gentle touch, like softest rain.

In the garden, colors blend,
Nature's brush, a perfect friend.
Each petal opens to the light,
Whispers of morning, pure delight.

A breeze stirs leaves with tender grace,
As sunlight kisses every face.
The world exhales a hopeful sigh,
In this moment, I can fly.

Time slows down, the heart unwinds,
In quiet wonder, peace we find.
Life's simple joys, a cherished rite,
In the beauty of morning light.

Beneath the sky, our dreams take form,
In whispers soft, love's gentle storm.
This brand new day, a wondrous sight,
Whispers of morning, pure and bright.

Silken Elevation

A tapestry of dreams unfurled,
In silken threads, a vivid world.
With every stroke, the heart inspires,
To climb the peaks, ignite the fires.

As daylight breaks, the colors stream,
We rise together, pulse and beam.
In harmony, our spirits grow,
Through silken paths, we learn to flow.

Each moment stitched in time's embrace,
Through vibrant hues, we find our place.
In gentle whispers, love's invitation,
With every step, a new creation.

The heights we reach, a sacred vow,
In clouds of dreams, we rise somehow.
Elation sings in every breath,
In silken heights, we conquer death.

Through winding trails, our spirits soar,
In silken dreams, we crave for more.
Together we find our elevation,
In love's embrace, our celebration.

Soft Footsteps Forward

With gentle steps, I tread the ground,
In every heartbeat, wisdom found.
A path unmarked, but clear my aim,
Each footfall whispers, soft as flame.

Through fields of gold, through valleys wide,
In every corner, hope and pride.
The journey's long, but spirit bright,
With soft footsteps, I chase the light.

In shadows deep, where doubts may creep,
I find my strength, my soul will leap.
With every step, I'll leave behind,
The heavy chains that once defined.

Through trials faced and dreams pursued,
I walk in faith, my heart imbued.
With open arms, the world ignites,
In soft footsteps, I find new heights.

Together we rise, hand in hand,
In gentle strides, we make our stand.
With love as guide, to seal our fate,
In soft footsteps forward, we create.

Milton Keynes UK
Ingram Content Group UK Ltd.
UKHW021630011224
451755UK00010B/540